The Wonder Weeks

Baby's First Year Diary

This diary belongs to:

The Wonder Weeks Leaps

With every developmental leap you make, you gain a new perceptive ability. That new ability enables you to sense, comprehend, enact, or perceive something new. With these new cognitive skills, your whole life changes over and over again. It's as if you have to rediscover the world anew! Each leap has three phases.

Phase 1: Fussiness

Making a developmental leap is an intense experience. So many changes! The first part of it consists of the fussiness phase, which signals the onset of a leap. Characteristic behaviors during this phase include clinginess, crankiness, and crying, or the Three Cs.

Phase 2: The Magical Leap Forward

Once you conquer the shock of discovering a new aspect of the world, you start to explore. Your unique personality emerges as you grow.

Phase 3: After the Leap

After all those new perceptions and reactions, you experience a more relaxing period of relative peace. You become less clingy, requiring less constant attention, and once again you become a ray of sunshine. Unfortunately, this period of peace and quiet doesn't last long because growing up takes lots of hard work!

your Leap Chart

The Wonder Weeks leap calendar counts from baby's due date, not birth date, because the brain develops at the same rate, whether still in the womb or out in the world. Baby's birth date is all about cake, but the due date helps calculate mental development.

Your Due Date: _____

Your Birth Date: _____

0   1   2   3   4   5   6   7   weeks old

8   9   10   11   12   13   14   weeks old

15   16   17   18   19   20   21   weeks old

22   23   24   25   26   27   28   weeks old

I calculated your leaps by:

☐ Doing the math.

☐ Consulting The Wonder Weeks app.

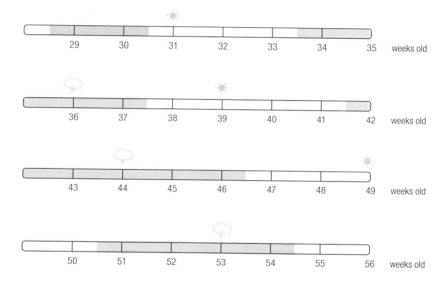

☐   You are going through a relatively uncomplicated phase.

☐   You may be fussier now.

☁   Around this week, you likely will have a "stormy" period.

☀   Around this week, your sunny side most likely will shine through.

▦   Irritable behavior around week 29 or 30 doesn't necessarily signal a leap. You're discovering that grownups can walk away and leave you behind. This is progress! You're learning a new skill: distances.

LEAP 1

Changing Sensations

AT 4 TO 5 WEEKS, YOUR SENSES ARE GROWING RAPIDLY, AND YOU INCREASINGLY SHOW INTEREST IN THE WORLD AROUND YOU. IT'S TIME FOR SOME ACTION!

This Leap's Fussy Phase

Date: _____

You are making your leap into the world of changing sensations. I noticed this because you:

_____

_____

_____

On a scale of fussiness, this leap is a:

☀   1   2   3   4   5   6   7   8   9   10   ☁

My cuddle care for you consists of:

_____

_____

_____

The top three ways to soothe you are:

1. _____

2. _____

3. _____

I feel:

_____

_____

_____

Your Three Cs

These were the changes in your

Clinginess:

_____

_____

Crankiness:

_____

_____

Crying:

_____

_____

and these were the changes in your

Sleeping:

_____

_____

Drinking:

_____

_____

Although making a leap can seem difficult, the fussy phase signals that progress is happening. The following pages reveal what I learned from your first leap.

Your Emotions

You show your emotions in different ways:

_____

_____

_____

_____

_____

_____

You smile when:

_____

_____

_____

_____

_____

_____

These are the physical changes in your breathing, burping, startling, trembling, crying, and vomiting:

_____

_____

_____

_____

_____

_____

Your Eyes

You like to look at these objects. They mean the world to you right now.

☐ You look at objects for longer periods and with more interest now.

☐ You like to look at the same objects over and over again.

☐ The brighter the object, the more interesting it seems to you.

☐ You get bored easily, and you want to see new objects every time.

Your Sounds & Touches

You like these sounds the most:

_____

_____

_____

These sounds scare you:

_____

_____

_____

You make these sounds:

_____

_____

_____

These are the ways that you like to be touched:

_____

_____

_____

These are the ways that you don't like being touched:

_____

_____

_____

Your Special Activities

You like to do these activities most:

_____

_____

_____

With _____ , your favorite activities include:

_____

_____

_____

With _____ , you like to:

_____

_____

_____

You indicate that you want a break by

☐ looking away for a moment.

☐ closing your eyes.

☐ turning your head.

☐ starting to cry.

☐ Other: _____

Your First Sensations

There's a first for everything! During the leap of changing sensations, these were some of your firsts:

First

_____

_____

_____

First

_____

_____

_____

First

_____

_____

_____

First

_____

_____

_____

First

_____

_____

_____

your Mighty Milestones

In the world of changing sensations, these are some of the milestones that you achieved:

Milestone 1

_____

_____

Milestone 2

_____

_____

Milestone 3

_____

_____

Milestone 4

_____

_____

Milestone 5

_____

_____

Date of your first real smile: _____

Date of your first real tear: _____

Special Memories

Your First Letter from Me!

Dear

Love,

Congratulations!

You Made Your Leap of Changing Sensations!

Your handprint:

Date: _____

Height: _____

Weight: _____

Notes

Your Scrapbook of Changing Sensations

What best represents this leap? Keep
special memorabilia here, including
cards, drawings, notes, and photos.

Patterns

BETWEEN WEEKS 7 AND 9, YOU DEVELOP THE ABILITY TO
RECOGNIZE SIMPLE PATTERNS IN YOUR OWN BODY AND IN
THE WORLD AROUND YOU. IT'S A WHOLE NEW WORLD!

This Leap's Fussy Phase

Date: _____

You are making your leap into the world of patterns. I noticed this because you:

_____

_____

_____

On a scale of fussiness, this leap is a:

☀   1   2   3   4   5   6   7   8   9   10   ⚡

My cuddle care for you consists of:

_____

_____

_____

The top three ways to soothe you are:

1. _____

2. _____

3. _____

I feel:

_____

_____

_____

Your Three Cs

These were the changes in your

Clinginess:

_____

_____

Crankiness:

_____

_____

Crying:

_____

_____

and these were the changes in your

Sleeping:

_____

_____

Drinking:

_____

_____

You
- [ ] slept poorly.
- [ ] cried, cried, and cried some more.
- [ ] clung to me more tightly.
- [ ] wanted more attention.
- [ ] became shy with strangers.

Your Body

You move in these different ways:

_____

_____

_____

With your body, now you can:

_____

_____

_____

With your hands, you:

_____

_____

_____

You discovered these body parts:

_____

_____

_____

You looked closely and also saw:

_____

_____

_____

_____

Visual Patterns

Patterns are everywhere! Of all the patterns around you, you love these the most:

Your Eyes

You now move and use your eyes in these different ways:

_____

_____

_____

_____

When we walk around, you look at:

_____

_____

_____

_____

Your favorite person to see is:

_____

_____

_____

_____

You love watching

☐ flickering lights.

☐ waving curtains.

☐ shiny jewelry or clothing.

☐ pets moving or eating.

☐ people moving or eating.

Your Listening & Sounds

You react to sounds differently now by:

_____

_____

_____

_____

_____

You like to listen to:

_____

_____

_____

_____

_____

These new sounds scare you:

_____

_____

_____

_____

_____

You make these new sounds:

_____

_____

_____

_____

_____

Your Play

The toys you love the most are:

_____

_____

_____

_____

_____

You love to investigate or play with these non-toy objects at home:

_____

_____

_____

_____

You love to investigate or play with these non-toy objects outside home:

_____

_____

_____

_____

_____

You prefer

☐ toys.

☐ "real" objects.

Your Special Activities

You like to do these activities most:

_____

_____

_____

_____

_____

With _____ , your favorite activities include:

_____

_____

_____

_____

With _____ , you like to:

_____

_____

_____

_____

your Games, Songs & Faces

You like to play these games:

_____

_____

_____

_____

_____

Some of the songs I sing for you include:

_____

_____

_____

_____

_____

I love these different faces that you make:

_____

_____

_____

_____

_____

So Typically you!

These words best describe you and your character now:

_____

_____

_____

_____

The best (most awesome, beautiful, or funny) comment that someone made about you:

_____

_____

_____

_____

When I talk to you, I tell you:

_____

_____

_____

_____

When you "talk" back, you're telling me:

_____

_____

_____

_____

This is what I'm learning from you:

_____

_____

_____

_____

Your First Patterns

There's a first for everything! During the leap of patterns, these were some of your firsts:

First

_____

_____

_____

First

_____

_____

_____

First

_____

_____

_____

First

_____

_____

_____

First

_____

_____

_____

Your Mighty Milestones

In the world of patterns, you achieved these milestones:

Milestone 1

_____

_____

_____

Milestone 2

_____

_____

_____

Milestone 3

_____

_____

_____

Milestone 4

_____

_____

_____

Milestone 5

_____

_____

_____

Special Memories

Your Second Letter from Me!

Dear

Love,

Congratulations!

You Made Your Leap of Patterns!

Your handprint:

Date: _____

Height: _____

Weight: _____

Notes

Your Scrapbook of Patterns

What best represents this leap? Keep special memorabilia here, including cards, drawings, notes, and photos.

Smooth Transitions

AT 11 TO 12 WEEKS, YOU RECOGNIZE SMOOTH TRANSITIONS
IN SIGHTS, SOUNDS, SMELLS, TASTES, AND TOUCH.
WITH THIS NEW ABILITY, NOT ONLY CAN YOU REGISTER
THESE TRANSITIONS WHEN SOMEONE ELSE DOES
THEM, BUT YOU ALSO CAN DO THEM ON YOUR OWN!

This Leap's Fussy Phase

Date: _____

You are making your leap into the world of changing sensations. I noticed this because you:

_____

_____

_____

On a scale of fussiness, this leap is a:

☀   1   2   3   4   5   6   7   8   9   10   ☁

My cuddle care for you consists of:

_____

_____

_____

The top three ways to soothe you are:

1. _____

2. _____

3. _____

I feel:

_____

_____

_____

Your Three Cs

These were the changes in your
Clinginess:

_____

_____

Crankiness:

_____

_____

Crying:

_____

_____

and these were the changes in your
Sleeping:

_____

_____

Drinking:

_____

_____

You
- ☐ slept poorly.
- ☐ lost your appetite.
- ☐ were inactive.
- ☐ sucked your thumb more often.
- ☐ clung to me more tightly.
- ☐ became shy with strangers.

Your Body Control

Your control of your body has changed in these ways:

_____

_____

_____

_____

You like to move your body in these ways:

_____

_____

_____

_____

You move more smoothly in these ways:

_____

_____

_____

_____

You roll or hold your head straight when:

_____

_____

_____

_____

Your Hands & Touches

When you discovered your own hands, you:

_____

_____

_____

_____

With your hands, you most like to:

_____

_____

_____

_____

If you touch your own face, you:

_____

_____

_____

_____

If you touch my face, you:

_____

_____

_____

_____

Your Eyes

Your eyes now follow objects in a controlled, coordinated manner.

When you look at my face, you focus on:

_____

_____

_____

You like to see smooth transitions around you, such as

☐ lights dimming or brightening.

☐ a hand moving.

☐ a head turning.

☐ a toy operating.

☐ Other: _____

Your Emotions & Behaviors

You express your enjoyment by

☐ watching or looking.

☐ listening.

☐ making a sound and waiting for a response.

☐ grabbing.

☐ Other: _____

You show that you're bored by:

_____

_____

_____

_____

Your other new emotions include:

_____

_____

_____

_____

You express these different behaviors around different people:

_____

_____

_____

_____

Your Sounds

More smoothly than before, you like to

☐ make vowel sounds.

☐ gurgle.

☐ shriek.

These are the sounds you make and when and where you make them:

_____

_____

_____

If I imitate your sounds, you:

_____

_____

_____

When I talk to you, I tell you:

_____

_____

_____

When you "talk" back, you're telling me:

_____

_____

_____

You laugh when:

_____

_____

_____

your Music & Play

The music that you like most now includes:

_____

_____

_____

As a way of exploring the world, you like to touch:

_____

_____

_____

The toys that you love most are:

_____

_____

_____

You love to investigate or play with these non-toy objects at home:

_____

_____

_____

You love to investigate or play with these non-toy objects outside home:

_____

_____

_____

Your First Smooth Transitions

There's a first for everything! During the leap of smooth transitions, these were some of your firsts:

First

_____

_____

_____

First

_____

_____

_____

First

_____

_____

_____

First

_____

_____

_____

First

_____

_____

_____

Your Mighty Milestones

In the world of smooth transitions, you achieved these milestones:

Milestone 1

_____
_____
_____

Milestone 2

_____
_____
_____

Milestone 3

_____
_____
_____

Milestone 4

_____
_____
_____

Milestone 5

_____
_____
_____

Special Memories

Your Third Letter from Me!

Dear

Love,

Congratulations!

You Made Your Leap of Smooth Transitions!

Your handprint:

Date: _____

Height: _____

Weight: _____

Notes

Your Scrapbook of Smooth Transitions

What best represents this leap? Keep special memorabilia here, including cards, drawings, notes, and photos.

LEAP 4

Events

AROUND 19 WEEKS, YOU BEGIN TO EXPERIMENT WITH EVENTS.
THE WORD "EVENTS" DOESN'T MEAN SPECIAL OCCASIONS.
HERE IT DENOTES A SHORT, FAMILIAR SEQUENCE OF
SMOOTH TRANSITIONS FROM ONE PATTERN TO THE NEXT.

This Leap's Fussy Phase

Date: _____

You are making your leap into the world of events. I noticed this because you:

_____

_____

_____

On a scale of fussiness, this leap is a:

☀   1   2   3   4   5   6   7   8   9   10   ☁

My cuddle care for you consists of:

_____

_____

_____

The top three ways to soothe you are:

1. _____

2. _____

3. _____

I feel:

_____

_____

_____

Your Three Cs

These were the changes in your
Clinginess:

_____

_____

Crankiness:

_____

_____

Crying:

_____

_____

and these were the changes in your
Sleeping:

_____

_____

Drinking:

_____

_____

You
- ☐ had trouble sleeping.
- ☐ lost your appetite.
- ☐ were inactive.
- ☐ were moody.
- ☐ needed more head support.
- ☐ demanded more attention.
- ☐ always wanted to be with me.
- ☐ became shy with strangers.

your Exploration

You are perceiving the world in a different way than before this leap. This is what I'm noticing:

_____

_____

_____

_____

_____

_____

_____

_____

_____

_____

_____

_____

_____

_____

_____

_____

_____

_____

_____

_____

_____

_____

_____

_____

Your Way of Examining

You now can make coordinated, flowing movements.

As a result, you
- ☐ reach for
- ☐ grab
- ☐ pull

toys toward yourself in one smooth movement to examine them.

You like to examine objects by
- ☐ poking them.
- ☐ turning them around.
- ☐ sliding them up and down.
- ☐ shaking them.
- ☐ banging them.
- ☐ putting them in your mouth.

LEAP 4

When you examine something new, you often make these movements:

_____

_____

This is what you like to examine with your mouth:

Your Observations

Sometimes you observe me. For example:

_____

_____

_____

_____

_____

Sometimes you become too tired to continue observing. I help you by:

_____

_____

_____

_____

_____

You show keen interest in certain objects or details, especially:

_____

_____

_____

_____

_____

Your favorite observations include:

_____

_____

_____

_____

_____

your Sight & Seeing

Of everything that we do every day, your favorite activity or object to watch is:

_____

_____

_____

_____

You can't read yet, but if I show you a colorful image, you:

_____

_____

_____

_____

If you look in a mirror or see me in a mirror, you:

_____

_____

_____

_____

You love watching these repetitive activities (jumping up and down, brushing hair, cutting food) the most:

_____

_____

_____

_____

_____

Your Sounds

You are stringing together babbling sounds, almost like a sentence. Lately you "tell" me:

_____

_____

_____

This is how you experiment with intonation and volume:

_____

_____

_____

You're making new sounds with your lips and tongue. They sound like:

- ☐ Arrr
- ☐ Brrr
- ☐ Ffft-ffft-ffft
- ☐ Grrr
- ☐ Prrr
- ☐ Rrr
- ☐ Sss
- ☐ Vvv
- ☐ Zzz

If you cough and I cough back, you:

_____

_____

_____

_____

Your Body Control & Movements

The new movements that you can make after this leap include:

_____
_____
_____
_____

You "ask" me to pick you up by:

_____
_____
_____
_____

LEAP 4

When I put you on the floor, you:

_____
_____
_____
_____

You can

☐ grab objects with either hand.

☐ grab an object if your hand touches it, even without looking.

☐ pass objects from one hand to another.

☐ shake your toys.

☐ bang your toys on surfaces.

☐ deliberately throw objects on the floor.

Your Mouth & Eating

With your tongue, you like to:

_____

_____

_____

_____

When you're hungry, you:

_____

_____

_____

_____

When you've had enough to eat, you:

_____

_____

_____

_____

With my mouth, you like to:

_____

_____

_____

_____

Your Special Activities

You like to do these activities most:

_____

_____

_____

_____

_____

_____

With _____ , your favorite activities include:

_____

_____

_____

_____

_____

_____

With _____ , you like to:

_____

_____

_____

_____

_____

_____

_____

So Typically You!

These words best describe you and your character now:

_____

_____

_____

_____

The best (most awesome, beautiful, or funny) comment that someone made about you:

_____

_____

_____

_____

When I talk to you, I tell you:

_____

_____

_____

When you "talk" back, you're telling me:

_____

_____

_____

This is what I'm learning from you:

_____

_____

_____

your First Events

There's a first for everything! During the leap of events, some of your firsts included:

First

_____

_____

_____

First

_____

_____

_____

First

_____

_____

_____

First

_____

_____

_____

First

_____

_____

_____

your Mighty Milestones

In the world of events, you achieved these milestones:

Milestone 1

_____

_____

_____

Milestone 2

_____

_____

_____

Milestone 3

_____

_____

_____

Milestone 4

_____

_____

_____

Milestone 5

_____

_____

_____

Special Memories

Your Fourth Letter from Me!

Dear

Love,

Congratulations!

You Made Your Leap of Events!

Your handprint:

Date: _____

Height: _____

Weight: _____

Your Scrapbook of Events

What best represents this leap? Keep special memorabilia here, including cards, drawings, notes, and photos.

Relationships

BETWEEN WEEKS 25 AND 27, YOU USE YOUR KNOWLEDGE OF
EVENTS AS A FOUNDATION TO UNDERSTAND THE RELATIONSHIPS
AMONG THE OBJECTS IN THE WORLD. THE MORE YOU ENGAGE
WITH DIFFERENT SIGHTS, SOUNDS, SMELLS, TASTES, AND
TOUCHES, THE BETTER YOUR UNDERSTANDING WILL BE.

This Leap's Fussy Phase

Date: _____

You are making your leap into the world of relationships. I noticed this because you:

_____

_____

_____

On a scale of fussiness, this leap is a:

☀️　　1　　2　　3　　4　　5　　6　　7　　8　　9　　10　　⛈️

My cuddle care for you consists of:

_____

_____

_____

The top three ways to soothe you are:

1. _____

2. _____

3. _____

I feel:

_____

_____

_____

_____

Your Three Cs

These were the changes in your
Clinginess:

_____

_____

Crankiness:

_____

_____

Crying:

_____

_____

and these were the changes in your
Sleeping:

_____

_____

Drinking:

_____

_____

You
- ☐ were inactive.
- ☐ were quieter and less vocal.
- ☐ lost your appetite.
- ☐ had nightmares.
- ☐ didn't want me to change your diaper.
- ☐ reached for cuddly objects more often.
- ☐ always wanted to be with me.
- ☐ wanted me to keep you busy.

Your Exploration

You are perceiving the world in a different way than before this leap. This is what I'm noticing:

_____

_____

_____

_____

_____

_____

_____

_____

_____

_____

_____

_____

_____

_____

_____

_____

_____

_____

_____

_____

_____

_____

Your Distances

In, out, in front of, behind, and next to are important perceptions in this leap. This is how you're experimenting with these concepts:

_____

_____

_____

_____

The two objects you most like to put in and out of each other are:

_____

_____

_____

_____

You explore the concept of distance by:

_____

_____

_____

_____

If I walk away, enlarging the distance between us, you:

_____

_____

_____

_____

your Actions & Reactions

You're playing with relationships, and you love experimenting with them. You've discovered these buttons and switches that you like to flip:

_____

_____

You realize that you can take apart objects, including your toys. You like to take apart:

_____

_____

You show tremendous interest in examining

- ☐ buttons.
- ☐ labels.
- ☐ marks on the wall.
- ☐ screws.
- ☐ stickers.
- ☐ zippers
- ☐ Other: _____

Here you are playing with a little detail:

Your Body

This is how you use your hands to grab:

_____

_____

_____

_____

_____

You like to lift _____ to look under it. When you do, you:

_____

_____

_____

_____

_____

You mimic these gestures:

_____

_____

_____

_____

_____

If you get your hands on a ball, you:

_____

_____

_____

_____

_____

Your Sight & Seeing

When you observe adults, you like to look at:

_____

_____

_____

_____

_____

_____

The animal you like to watch most is:

_____

_____

_____

_____

_____

_____

This is how you look from one object to another:

_____

_____

_____

_____

_____

Your Smile

If someone does something that interests you, you:

_____

_____

_____

_____

_____

When I do something by accident, like drop an object on the ground, you:

_____

_____

_____

_____

_____

You laugh hard when you see:

_____

_____

_____

_____

_____

Your Listening & Sounds

When you hear music, this is how your body responds:

_____

_____

_____

When you hear voices or sounds coming from my phone, you:

_____

_____

_____

You're making connections between words and their meaning! I can see you understand phrases such as:

☐ "No, don't do that."

☐ "Come on, let's go."

☐ _____

You're trying to say words. When you "talk," you're trying to say:

_____

_____

_____

Your First Six Months

You're my mini-me in these ways:

_____
_____
_____
_____
_____
_____
_____
_____
_____
_____
_____
_____
_____
_____
_____
_____
_____
_____
_____
_____
_____
_____

months

Your Special Activities

You like to do these activities most:

_____

_____

_____

_____

_____

_____

_____

With _____ , your favorite activities include:

_____

_____

_____

_____

_____

With _____ , you like to:

_____

_____

_____

_____

_____

_____

Your Mighty Milestones

In the world of relationships, you achieved these milestones:

Milestone 1

_____

_____

_____

Milestone 2

_____

_____

_____

Milestone 3

_____

_____

_____

Milestone 4

_____

_____

_____

Milestone 5

_____

_____

_____

_____

_____

Special Memories

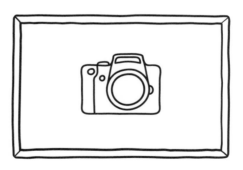

Your Fifth Letter from Me!

Dear

Love,

You Made Your Leap of Relationships!

Your handprint:

Date: _____

Height: _____

Weight: _____

Notes

Your Scrapbook of Relationships

What best represents this leap? Keep special memorabilia here, including cards, drawings, notes, and photos.

LEAP 6

Categories

AT AROUND 37 WEEKS, YOUR UNDERSTANDING OF
THE WORLD BECOMES MORE SPECIFIC, AND YOU CAN
CLASSIFY THE WORLD INTO GROUPS. YOU'RE LEARNING
THAT DIFFERENT OBJECTS SHARE THE SAME TRAITS!

This Leap's Fussy Phase

Date: _____

You are making your leap into the world of categories. I noticed this because you:

_____

_____

_____

On a scale of fussiness, this leap is a:

☀   1   2   3   4   5   6   7   8   9   10   ☁

My cuddle care for you consists of:

_____

_____

_____

The top three ways to soothe you are:

1. _____

2. _____

3. _____

I feel:

_____

_____

_____

Your Three Cs

These were the changes in your

Clinginess:

_____

_____

Crankiness:

_____

_____

Crying:

_____

_____

and these were the changes in your

Sleeping:

_____

_____

Drinking:

_____

_____

You
- [ ] were inactive.
- [ ] were shy.
- [ ] were less lively.
- [ ] babbled less.
- [ ] had nightmares.
- [ ] acted extra sweet.
- [ ] refused to let your diaper be changed.
- [ ] clung to my clothes.
- [ ] held on to me tightly.
- [ ] demanded more attention.

Your Memory

You show that you recognize a specific object, such as an animal or person, by:

_____

_____

_____

_____

This is how you recognize and imitate the expressions and movements of people:

_____

_____

_____

_____

When I ask you where the _____ is in the book, this is how you point it out:

_____

_____

_____

_____

You know when something is dirty. You show this by:

_____

_____

_____

_____

Your Emotions

When you look in the mirror, you:

_____

_____

_____

_____

_____

If I pay attention to someone else, you:

_____

_____

_____

_____

_____

When your favorite toy falls, you:

_____

_____

_____

_____

_____

When you hear another child crying, you:

_____

_____

_____

_____

_____

Your Role Reversals

You try to switch roles by

☐ giving your bottle to me.

☐ asking me to sing a song and then clapping your hands.

☐ handing me blocks to build something.

☐ playing peek-a-boo with another baby.

☐ Other: _____

This is a story about the first time you showed me that you wanted to switch roles:

_____

_____

_____

_____

_____

_____

_____

_____

_____

_____

_____

_____

_____

_____

_____

_____

Discovering Categories

You're using your understanding of relationships to explore your ability to perceive and make categories, or groups of objects with the same characteristics.

You like to explore these categories in humans:

_____

_____

_____

You like to explore these categories with your toys:

_____

_____

_____

You like to explore these categories at home:

_____

_____

_____

_____

You explore categories of sensations, such as roughness, slipperiness, stickiness, or warmth, by:

_____

_____

_____

Your Sounds & Laughing

These are the different sounds you make for different people:

_____

_____

_____

_____

_____

_____

You clearly understand these words:

_____

_____

_____

_____

_____

_____

What makes you laugh most is:

_____

_____

_____

_____

_____

_____

Your Examinations

Inside, you love to examine:

_____

_____

_____

_____

_____

Outside, you love to examine:

_____

_____

_____

_____

_____

With _____ , you like to examine:

_____

_____

_____

_____

_____

When something falls or breaks apart, you like to examine:

_____

_____

_____

_____

_____

Your Special Activities

You like to do these activities most:

_____

_____

_____

_____

_____

_____

With _____ , your favorite activities include:

_____

_____

_____

_____

_____

_____

With _____ , you like to:

_____

_____

_____

_____

_____

_____

So Typically you!

These words best describe you and your character now:

_____

_____

_____

The best (most awesome, beautiful, or funny) comment that someone made about you:

_____

_____

_____

When I talk to you, I tell you:

_____

_____

_____

When you "talk" back, you're telling me:

_____

_____

_____

This is what I'm learning from you:

_____

_____

_____

_____

_____

your Mighty Milestones

In the world of categories, you achieved these milestones:

Milestone 1

_____

_____

_____

Milestone 2

_____

_____

_____

Milestone 3

_____

_____

_____

Milestone 4

_____

_____

_____

Milestone 5

_____

_____

_____

Special Memories

LEAP 6

Your Sixth Letter from Me!

Dear

Love,

Congratulations!

You Made Your Leap of Categories!

Your handprint:

Date: _____

Height: _____

Weight: _____

Your Scrapbook of Categories

What best represents this leap? Keep special memorabilia here, including cards, drawings, notes, and photos.

LEAP 7

Sequences

BETWEEN WEEKS 44 AND 48, YOU ARE ACTING IN
SEQUENCES, AND YOUR ACTIONS BECOME MORE
PURPOSEFUL. YOU KNOW WHAT YOU'RE DOING!

This Leap's Fussy Phase

Date: _____

You are making your leap into the world of sequences. I noticed this because you:

_____

_____

_____

On a scale of fussiness, this leap is a:

☀ 1   2   3   4   5   6   7   8   9   10   ☁

My cuddle care for you consists of:

_____

_____

_____

The top three ways to soothe you are:

1. _____

2. _____

3. _____

I feel:

_____

_____

_____

your Three Cs

These were the changes in your

Clinginess:

_____

_____

Crankiness:

_____

_____

Crying:

_____

_____

and these were the changes in your

Sleeping:

_____

_____

Drinking:

_____

_____

You
- ☐ were inactive.
- ☐ sat quietly.
- ☐ lost your appetite.
- ☐ babbled less.
- ☐ were shy around others.
- ☐ refused to let your diaper be changed.
- ☐ behaved more babyish.
- ☐ sucked your thumb more often.
- ☐ cuddled your toys more often.
- ☐ wanted to stay busy.
- ☐ were jealous.
- ☐ were crying one moment, cheerful the next.
- ☐ acted unusually sweet.

LEAP 7

Your Pointing & Talking

When I say the name of someone near you, you:

_____

_____

_____

When I ask you where your _____ is, you:

_____

_____

_____

You ask me to tell you the names of objects, animals, and people by:

_____

_____

_____

You make these sounds now:

_____

_____

_____

When I ask you what sound your favorite animal makes, you make this sound:

_____

_____

_____

_____

Your Activities

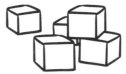

When I switch on a light, you:

_____

_____

_____

_____

When I give you a key, you:

_____

_____

_____

_____

When I give you blocks, you:

_____

_____

_____

_____

When I put you in a sandbox with a small shovel, you:

_____

_____

_____

_____

Your Goal-Reaching Skills

When you want me to take you in a specific direction, you:

_____

_____

_____

_____

_____

_____

If you can't reach something, you:

_____

_____

_____

_____

_____

_____

When you try to get up or "walk" around, you:

_____

_____

_____

_____

_____

Your Sequences

You're becoming aware that you need to perform actions in a specific order to reach a goal. Here are some sequences that you do:

First, you   Then, you

_____   _____

_____   _____

_____   _____

_____   _____

_____   _____

_____   _____

_____   _____

_____   _____

_____   _____

_____   _____

_____   _____

_____   _____

_____   _____

_____   _____

_____   _____

_____   _____

_____   _____

_____   _____

Your Constructions

The first time I saw you putting objects together, you:

_____

_____

_____

_____

_____

The first thing you constructed was:

_____

_____

_____

_____

_____

This is how you like to construct, link, or combine objects:

_____

_____

_____

_____

_____

Your Eating

You want
- ☐ me to feed you.
- ☐ to feed yourself.

When you eat, you:

_____

_____

_____

_____

_____

You want to share your food with:

_____

_____

_____

_____

_____

If I give you a spoon and your food, you:

_____

_____

_____

_____

_____

LEAP 7

Your Special Activities

You like to do these activities most:

_____

_____

_____

_____

_____

_____

With _____ , your favorite activities include:

_____

_____

_____

_____

_____

With _____ , you like to:

_____

_____

_____

_____

_____

_____

Your Games & Toys

Your favorite nursery rhyme is:

_____

_____

_____

_____

When you hear it, you:

_____

_____

_____

_____

Your most loved toys are:

_____

_____

_____

_____

These are some of your other favorites:

_____

_____

_____

_____

Your First Sequences

There's a first for everything! During the leap of sequences, some of your firsts included:

First

_____

_____

_____

First

_____

_____

_____

First

_____

_____

_____

First

_____

_____

_____

First

_____

_____

_____

Your Mighty Milestones

In the world of sequences, you achieved these milestones:

Milestone 1

_____

_____

_____

Milestone 2

_____

_____

_____

Milestone 3

_____

_____

_____

Milestone 4

_____

_____

_____

Milestone 5

_____

_____

_____

Special Memories

Your Seventh Letter from Me!

Dear

Love,

Congratulations!

You Made Your Leap of Sequences!

Your handprint:

Date: _____

Height: _____

Weight: _____

Notes

LEAP 7

your Scrapbook of Sequences

What best represents this leap? Keep special memorabilia here, including cards, drawings, notes, and photos.

Programs

BETWEEN WEEKS 50 AND 55, YOU'RE LEARNING TO "PLAY" WITH MAKING DIFFERENT CHOICES AND DISCOVERING THEIR CONSEQUENCES. A PROGRAM CONSISTS OF A SEQUENCE OF ACTIONS THAT DON'T HAVE A PRESCRIBED ORDER, SUCH AS BUILDING A TOWER OF BLOCKS OR GETTING DRESSED. YOU CAN REACH THE GOAL IN ANY NUMBER OF WAYS. IT'S TIME TO EXPERIMENT!

Happy First Birthday!

These people came to celebrate your special day with you:

_____

_____

_____

_____

_____

_____

_____

_____

_____

_____

_____

You received these special presents:

_____

_____

_____

_____

_____

_____

_____

_____

_____

_____

_____

On your day in the spotlight, you:

_____

_____

_____

_____

_____

_____

_____

_____

_____

_____

_____

_____

_____

_____

_____

_____

_____

_____

_____

_____

_____

_____

Also available from
THE WONDER WEEKS:

The Wonder Weeks

A Stress-Free Guide to Your

Baby's Behavior

The Wonder Weeks:

Back to You

The Ultimate Recovery

Program After Pregnancy

For information about permission to reproduce selections from this book, write to Permissions, Countryman Press, 500 Fifth Avenue, New York, NY 10110

For information about special discounts for bulk purchases, please contact W. W. Norton Special Sales at specialsales@wwnorton.com or 800-233-4830

Manufacturing by Toppan Leefung Pte. Ltd.

Countryman Press

www.countrymanpress.com

An imprint of W. W. Norton & Company, Inc.

500 Fifth Avenue, New York, NY 10110

www.wwnorton.com

978-1-68268-720-8

10 9 8 7 6 5 4 3 2 1